ENGULFED

APURVA PRAKASH

Made with ♥ on the Notion Press Platform
www.notionpress.com

To everyone

who has faced the havoc within

Contents

Contents

Contents

wait for the cycle to complete,

wait a while for the light.

Foreword

In the quiet corners of our minds, where shadows linger and whispers of doubt echo, lies a world many fear to confront. Engulfed invites you into that world—not as a mere observer but as a traveler through the labyrinth of raw emotions, unspoken struggles, and the fragile feelings of humans.

This collection of poetry is more than words on a page; it is a mirror reflecting the darkness we often hide from ourselves and others. It dares to explore the depths of despair, the weight of hopelessness, and the silent wars waged within. Yet, amid this darkness, there are glimmers of resilience—a testament to the strength it takes to survive when the mind becomes a battlefield.

Engulfed does not promise comfort or answers, but it offers connection. It is for those who have felt the grip of overwhelming emotions, for those who have struggled to find their voice, and for those who seek solace in knowing they are not alone.

This book is a reminder that even in the darkest of times, there is value in bearing witness to the truth of our experiences. It is a space to feel, to grieve, and, perhaps, to heal.

As you turn these pages, may you find not only the weight of shared pain but also the strength that comes from acknowledging it. Welcome to Engulfed—a journey into the soul's deepest shadows, where even the darkness has its poetry.

Preface

Engulfed was born from the depths of my own mind—a place where silence often grows deafening, and the weight of unspoken struggles feels inescapable. It is a reflection of countless nights spent wrestling with emotions too complex to articulate, yet too powerful to ignore.

This collection of poetry is my attempt to give shape to the intangible—to put into words the shadows that linger, the battles fought in isolation, and the moments of quiet resilience that emerge even in the darkest times. It is not a guide, nor does it seek to offer answers; instead, it serves as a companion for anyone who has ever felt consumed by their thoughts or overwhelmed by the weight of their mental health.

Writing Engulfed was both an act of catharsis and a journey of understanding. Through these poems, I sought not to escape the darkness, but to confront it—to embrace its lessons and acknowledge its role in shaping who I am. It is my hope that readers will find a sense of connection within these pages , whether in the struggles shared, the emotions explored, or the flickers of light that persist despite the surrounding shadows.

This book is for anyone who has ever felt lost in their own mind, for those who have faced their fears and survived, and for those still fighting to make sense of it all. May Engulfed remind you that you are not alone, and that even in the depths of struggle, there is strength in vulnerability and beauty in resilience.

APURVA.

Acknowledgements

I am deeply grateful to those who stood by me through my darkest moments, offering light,help and support.

To the readers who connect with these words, thank you for allowing my voice to echo in your world.

To those who listen, who care, and who choose to stay—you mean more than you know.

And to my past self, for holding on through the chaos—this is the testament to your strength.

Thank you for being a part of this journey.

1. DEAD END

This helical path
led me to this dead end
I was trying to escape

There's bright darkness and a loud silence
No one whispering anything in my ears anymore
I can't see the wrong they're doing to me
There's nothing to want
And nothing to give
All I know is I don't want to exist like this
Maybe this is the dead end
I was craving for
when I was afraid
Maybe this is the dead end I was running from
when I thought I was brave

2. TRAPPED

These endless dark alleys
Entraps me whole
I've been running for forever
But this darkness outruns my soul

3. MY HOME

The only thing I've yearned for
are pale yellow walls and
the afternoon sun hitting it.
The only thing I've yearned for
is the aroma of a place I used to call mine.
I miss the outgrown trees,
I miss those creaked windows.
I miss the asymmetries,
I miss that all not so perfect place I used to call home.
I've lived in skyscrapers
I've lived in the apartment
I've tried the mountains
and all the different terrains
But the only things I've yearned
is the house , on that old street in my homeland.
I miss those old dark rooms,
Those grayish cement stairs,
The creepy outhouse and
the cream plastic chairs.
I miss the garden where
I used to play hide and seek
I miss the backyard
where we used to grow
lemon and seasonal seeds.
I miss the noise and I miss the silence

I miss our shared moments of laughter
and sadness
I miss the wounds , I miss the chase
I miss evening homeworks and
early morning breads.
I miss the winters , bonfire and corn
I miss the summers ,ice cubes , coolers
and running along.
I miss my home and
the place from where I used to belong.

I wish to be there
but I'm afraid of the shot
I fear when I'll call out
there will no one from my past.

4. THERE'S NO HOME

There's no home,
No place to hide
No place to call my own
No person to share the roof
under which I lie
The echoes of yesterday
Is still afresh
And when I lie,
I dreamt of home that was never mine
I've walked a lot
Watched my passion and people died
Everything that ever mattered to me
Is nothing more than ashes and cry
Darkness clings to me like
My own shadow
In the void
When I search for the shore
With distant memories
And no hopes
Longing for a home forever more
Even if I walk forever
On the paths known
I'll never find the road
That leads me home

5. HALF-MASKS

I dive deep in my dark musings
Only to realize I could never fly
In that bright sky
I wear these half makes of lie
So I could look in the mirror
And smile
While I internally die
With this gnawing fear
That all those success were not really mine
A stark contrast that
Stirs my own mind
Everything that is True
feels like a lie

I feel like an illusion
In my own mind
An imposter who sits in crowd and lies

6. IT ENDED WITHOUT AN ENDING

It ended without
a sound , a whisper , a trace
you were there one moment
And then you were gone
Leaving my heart ablaze

The scent of lingering memories
were bittersweet and defeaning
Grieving felt wrong
because there was never an ending
I waited for forever
walking down the road of hopes
though feeling shattered
when I saw the milestones
Years have passed yet
I'm trapped in the cycle of grief and longing
I think it wasn't something
that should've ended without an ending

7. EMPTY DREAMS

These potent, empty dreams
Rings like a melancholic knell
In my head
With vivid memories
of my mistakes
That led my soul astrayed
I seek comfort
in these barren skies
As no stars chart my way
Those hauting distant chimes
Of decayed aspirations
Still honks away every dream
I dare to take
I'm too tired to
make peace with it
So I stand stagnant
while all of it
Peirces my body

8. THE EMPTY PAGE

Yearning to be unchained
These thoughts races my mind,
While I sit there and see
you with hopes dwelling my eyes
These empty pages in my hand
are mere reflection of my words to you
I didn't lie when I said
My feelings flow but my utterance is doomed!
These empty pages
Chains my neck
Pulls me to liberation
And scares me to death
My voice confides in
These blank pages
A melody, a symphony or
These the hurtful rages

9. ANXITIES

It's all creeping back in
slowly and slowly,
making my heart race and
My palms sweat
I feel so alone ,
I feel so done
I wanna fall asleep
but I can't stop ,
the thoughts running in my mind
I wanna breathe, but it feels like someone's strangling my pipes
I wanna cry
but I'm afraid of how
I'll come off
I'm ashamed of how I feel
I'm embarrassed of how I think.

10. THE WEIGHT OF SECRETS

This weight of secrets
Breaks my back
Churns my heart
And make it black
These absolute truths
That I keep hiding
For the sake of myself and my sanity
Numbs my conscious
And pulls my head
Apart from my body

11. INVISBLE SCARS

These scars seep deep
The wounds drilled in my body
I see it all
I know why don't they like me

Every part of this existence
Is haunted
These invisible scars
Reins my judgements
No I see why I'm not wanted
These deep wounds
sollows me to my core
Wish I was good
Wish I could take it all
till it bores my bone

12. SILENT SCREAMS

In the silence of harms
Is where I'm residing
Take a look at me
you know I'm fighting
I weep everyday
And mask my sight
I scream silently
And bask my frights
I keep suffering in
The broad daylight

I've asked for help enough times
I hope someone notices
these silent screams
Like they notice my secret smile

13. SKELETON

These endless nights
Of miseries
Makes my soul
wail internally
This grief is growing
In my spine and marrow exponentially
I hear my own thoughts and
They settle in my nerves
like sediments
Maybe if I tear my skin up
I wouldn't be this sadness magnet
If I slit my wrist
Would it really help?
If I'll be this skeleton
Will it hurt a little less?

14. BACK TO THE CUPBOARD

Encore of past
In the way I dread
With half healed heart
And trauma ridden head
Alone in the crowd
Like the estranged kid
no friends , no family
No one to keep
Only to get swallowed by
Strangers with scavengers teeth
And then I felt like kid again
Who was used left and right
Nothing to adore and
Everything to fright
Who hoped to go away
So she'll never feel the pain
Even when she was already half past dead
She still lives
In the hope she'll never return
But there's no running away
I was her even on the best days

15. THE GREY SKY

Everyday repeats
To consume me and my rationality
These humrous bleak events
Wary's my body
Everyday I sit under this
Grey sky and craft lies
Paranoid and petrified by
my past and future combined

These eerily quiet grey sky
Makes my heart paint
These imageries of cognitive lies
I run in my dreams
to be away from myself
Just to fall again and
Find out it isn't yet the end!

16. HOPES TO THE ASHES

In the ruins of dreams
I stand still
My hopes burning
While I crawl through the
Wreckages of my dream
I'm part ruined
I'm part ruination
I've chased myself
In this effed up creation
I'm half ruined
I'm half ruination

17. THE WALLS I HAVE BUILT

These walls around me
touches the sky
and roots down to the core
I feel safe and protected here
From others
Until my thoughts bleed
me to death
And strangle me
till I gasp for my last breath
These walls I've built
Cages me from living
These walls I've built
eats me everyday
A little

18. DEPRESSIONAL EPISODES

I'm in the rut again,
With the same algorithm
And lizard brain.
My tremors shaking me,
Internally, there's a hurricane.
I've been sitting beside
My friends for a while,
And yet everything feels mundane.
Hobbies and chores feel alike,
I don't know what to love
And what to hate

19. I WISH

I hate that you don't remember me,
like I do.
I hate you don't try to find my face in strangers , like I do.
I hate that you don't think about me,
I hate all and every single possibility.
I just wish you remember me
,like I remember you.
I just wish all these words were not just mine but yours too.

20. PEOPLE DON'T FALL IN LOVE WITH PEOPLE LIKE ME

People don't fall in love
With people like me
Someone with a fractured heart
And shattered brain
They see me like a tragedy
Even if I tell them tales
And express my love with
All my shares
They'll never actually know
How much they mean to me
But to my despair
I'm always hyper aware
That people don't
Fall in love with
People like me

21. I WISH IT WERE ME

For once, just once, I wish it were me,
The girl he likes more than anything,
Like his brewed morning coffee,
And his afternoon sleep.
Like the pet he saved his money for when he was sixteen,
I wish he'd see me with the same passion
That roars within him when he watches movies.
I hope he'd run for/to me in the rain,
Just so we could drench together,
And afterward, make me his special canned soup
To make me feel better.
I wish every day were like that,
With him saving a seat for me all week.
For once, just once, I wish it were me,
The girl he likes more than anything.

22. BROKEN DREAMS

All I hear are broken dreams,
some shallow
some big ones shattered into pieces
Some that you walked halfway through
and some that you thought
were not worth it
Some with little rust
And a few that are now dusty
Some that you lost by whisker
and some that are still in your heart and you never got over.

23. WOUNDED SOUL

I'm here again
In the place where
My love and life died.
Through my own hands
I murdered everything
And called it a sacrifice
Even if I live forever now
I'll never be alive

24. BROKEN HOME

Drowned in the buzz of
This insanely silent house
I see through the windows
Waiting for the turmoils to knock
A heavy blow is all I hear
Before my thoughts strangled
Between everything I hold dear

That's when I realized
This is where I'll always belong
Standing in the doorways
Of a house
We wished was home

25. GHOST OF YOU

I danced my last night
With the ghost of you
We were singing at
the top of our lungs
Like we used to do
You danced me into delusions
Kissed me till I was stuck in hallucinations
You had me entirely
When I had this relevation

I danced my last night
With the ghost of you

26. IF I COULD

If I could go back
just One last time,
I'll sit my last night
With you, and
tell you my favorite tales
Of how you were
My first bestfriend
Even if I have to add
more moments to mourn
I'll live through it gladly
just to see you in flesh and bones
If I could go back
I'll ask you to stay
hold onto you
Like you held me
when I was born
for a little while more
while I weep and mourn
your pain.

27. I STILL LOVE YOU

In the dead of night
I see him again
swaying slowly
near the barricades
In my favorite
Iron maiden concert
Is this homage to my memories?
Or love that still hover between us
Does he still sings my favorite stanza
Like he loves it too
Or is it all just locked
In my long gone memory's tomb
I can still see him
Wearing the gloves I crocheted
He looks as handsome as ever
Under the lampshade
I wish this night could last forever
I've yet to savour him with all my heart
I wanna look at him forever
But I'm afraid this night is all I have

28. ALWAYS THE OTHER ONE

I know you always
Prefer her to me
Partly cause it's her
And partly cause you
Never loved me

Partly cause
She's that late October weather
In your favorite city
And partly cause
You never liked the rain
I bring
I know you'll always
Prefer her to me
Because I'm not the lover
You met on the Love Lock Bridge

29. I MISS YOU MORE

I'm missing you a little extra today
I want to see you from distance
Again and again
I want to wait for you
And defend your actions all the time
But how can I keep lying
When I'm sure I'm never on your mind
I dreamt of you last Night
We were together
Laughing , smiling and quarreling all the time
I like to think that someday we'll be this
But how can I deny the fact
That you already have someone to do this with you daily
I'm actively trying to give you up
Your thoughts, our past and every reminiscent I've got
But you float in my head
Like it's a free space
Hover over my mood
Like you've got the claim
I know even thinking this is not right
But lately you've been the reason
that makes me feel alive

30. SOMETIMES,MOST DAYS

Sometimes I feel so lost
Like I've lost everything
All the people,
All the purpose and
All the passion
I feel like everything
I ever did was a mistake
Like a failure , a shit

I don't wanna feel empty
While the panic and anxiety
Runs in my bones and streams
I don't wanna feel stranded
While these terror of nothingness kills me

31. ANXIETY

I feel my anxiety is white
It comes in all colors I know
Packed with sweats and dreads
to keep me low.
Sometimes it's red , filled with rage
Sometimes it's blue , filled with bereave
But my horror comes true
when it's yellow.
Making the happy things, feel shallow

32. HOME

Never knew what it felt like
But the longing to return was always there
I imagined it somewhat white
Giving it'll make me feel home
I can range all colors and emotions
Because it's my safe place
Where I'm not embarrassed to be mad , angry and sad
Where I'm not ashamed of how excited , happy and relieved I'm bout simple things
Where I can love selflessly, sing endlessly and cry uglily
I've been searching for it all my life
I've been yearning for it all my life
In places , in people and in myself

33. CRIPPLING LONLINESS

In the echoes of my emptiness
there's always a knock of silence
And the ray of darkness
Engulfing me little by little
through crippling lonliness

34. I CAN'T MOVE ON

I've let you go a thousand times
yet somehow I'm still here
waiting for you to come by
It's been years since you bid goodbye
and yet I'm here wasting my wishes
so I get a chance of saying "Hi"
I know what we had is in the past
And I also know that
 it was never ment to last
But I can never love anyone
Like I loved you
I might even find somcone better
But to my curse
in my heart and head
it's always going to be you

35. CAN'T LET YOU GO

You're no more here
Atleast not in the flesh and bone
I'm used to
I see your photo
Hung on that wall everyday
And all I feel is
how much there's left to say
You were my bestfriend,
You were my first person
And to let you go now
Without any last words
Is the biggest lost I've to suffer
I'm trying to let you go
Little by little
Somedays your loss doesn't hurt much
To know that you're not in pain anymore
Brings me peace too
But someday your loss pierce my heart
To know that you won't be there
In all the next phases of my life
Breaks me in parts
Your vibrant memories
Are fading everyday
But the pain of loosing you
Is not going away

I miss you so much
Much more than I've ever felt before
I think I'll miss you forever
Bleed my regrets over and over
I think I'll keep you with me
Until my time is over.

36. UNFINISHED-FINISHED?

The beauty of unfinished things
will always haunt the hope
Hope of maybes,
Hope of completion,
Hope of something more,
Just for a little more.
But the flip side,
is different than the
dreams , goals and fantasies
we knit.
More than the
things we want,
But less than what can fulfil us.
But these unfinished stories,
are more than the hopes,
more than the fantasies
It's a truth ,
something real ,
something more and something less
but something that gives you content
something for you, to end.
Sometimes the things that haunt us
are the things that can give us peace
Sometimes things that are unfinished,

Finishes me.

37. STRANGER IN THE MIRROR

I see this stranger in the mirror
She looks alike me
she looks happy and calm to look at
she doesn't look dreadful
Like how I feel
I see her smiling at things
Even when she's anxious
and on verge of insanity
She looks so similar
yet she's not me

38. THE VILLAIN OF STORY

I'm the villain of my own story
I mess everything
in the name of this forbidden glory
I push people away
sway alone in my thoughts of emptiness
I keep pushing things aside
until they pile up
And constrict all my nerves and pipes

39. FADING LIGHTS

An empty shell in the mirror
Hollow inside , eyes so clear
Hummings in the mind
"there's nothing to hold dear"
I see where I'm
in this room full of fears
Tears welding up
But my heart is at peace
Tremors and aches
Rotates in my body
I hate to see my reflections
in these little puddles
around me
Refusal is what now I seek
these breaths and pumps
are meek sense of win
is all I see

40. WISH IT GOES AWAY

For all I care
About the things
That are gone
I wish the memory
Seeps into the reality
So I cannot feel the loss

41. HE'D NEVER KNOW

He'd never know
I still search his name
In every call
He'd never know
I still sit and
daydream all my scars
He'll never know
I still wait for him
In our favorite bar
He'll never know
I'll always keep
Loving him from afar

42. HOPE WE MEET AGAIN

Hope we meet again
And spar like we did then
Go to our favorite bookshop
And play monopoly
While we sip wine and laugh
Hope we meet again
And this time you don't
Leave at 3 sharp
Eat those mochi
I prepared for you
And not forget me
 till this life or half
Hope I meet you again
Just to bid my bye
Hope we meet again
before our last rites

43. PHOTOS IN MY WALLET

These frozen times
In the back pocket
Of my jeans
Brings back the memories
Of the days when we were happy

When I ran to you
When I wanted to be home
But now I can only
See you through
Shades of colors
On a glossy paper
So I keep you close to me
And to feel your reminiscence physically
My wallet is built off
This memory tomb
Of everyone I've lost
whom I behold dearly.

44. THE SPACE BETWEEN US

I hope in this time
We were apart
You didn't outgrew me
And replaced my parts
This space that hovers
Between us hurts me too
I've been waiting for forever
To live our favorite time
And know each other like
We knew
I've been patiently aching
While I wait for you on this road
This space between us
Is vast and hollow
I hope you swim to me with
No sorrows

45. FOREVER IN LIMBO

I'm still smittend
 by the way you smile
Your lame jokes
And your half fried fries
I miss our comforting silence
And our small talks
The way I used to wait for your texts
And the way I used to
Die with a smile
When you passed my way
It's been four years
And I still stuck on you
With no hopes
And nothing new

46. MY LOVE FOR YOU IS ENDLESS

Even if tone it down
A hundred pixels
You'll always be my
Favorite picture
Even if I give up
All on my habits
You'll still be my
Sacred ritual
Even if I run out of
every drop of blood
My love for you
Will always be endless

47. THE WAY I AM

Trauma and pain intertwined
Wounds and scars makes my spine

48. NO STORIES TO TELL

There are no stories to tell
No hopes to dwell
I was stranded as a kid
With no history to tell

49. A FAILURE THROUGH AND THROUGH

My dreams and home
Love and hope
Lost everything I ever knew
I'm just a failure through and through

50. LOST IT ALL

Shards of me
Are scattered like my remains
Of dreams unfulfilled
And people that left me to be
With a heavy blow to my gut
I'm stranded on the sidewalk
With nowhere
To walk ahead

51. SCARRED AND INSENSITIVE

Oh, I'm so scarred,
that I feel ugly inside ,
My wounds are so deep
That meds go into voids
People gave me scars
and I collected it like stars
I thought it was badges to my bravery
and neglected my feelings
so I don't fall apart
And now they call me insensitive
because I'm not so empathetic

52. TRAGEDY

What a tragedy it is
to live in turmoil
And exist in peace
to give up on life
And still breathe

53. I RAN AWAY

I ran away,
when demons inside me
started killing the human
I built throughout those years
I ran away when I felt
I can't take anymore,
Living here.
I ran away ,
when I felt alone and dead inside
I ran away,
when my fears were the only thing
that made me feel alive
I ran away,
when the house I grew up in
started feeling like a
strange place.
I ran away,
to loose the pain
I ran away,
to be myself again.
I ran away,
to another state.
I ran away,
to be at home again

54. MEMORIES AND ME

Memories and me,
we lie in same grave
In the same beauty and pain,
In the same laughter and aches.
Memory and me
we lie in the same plane
living between the hurting and healing
running from the past
afraid of the forthcoming.
Memory and me
we are friends and foes
sometimes it makes me laugh
sometimes it cuts my heart into half
sometimes I create serene scenes for her
sometime I make her dread all the parts.

55. IF I DIE

If I die , it's voices in my head to blame
If I slit my wrist, it's hurt in my heart that's bleeding
If I die hanging , I was chocking on the painful memories
If I took poison , know the toxins were already in blood
If I jump off , know I was already trying to escape it all

56. DIED IN PIECES

Death in parts,
Like certain cacti,
Half of me gone,
Half still reactive.
The hope flickers,
While I dance between
Despair and resilience.
The depths of anxiety,
Make it hard to live with
This silence.
How morbidly poetic it is,
To have life and death intertwined.
Some parts of me are long gone,
While some still breathe and try.
But how long can I still breathe,
With nothing to gain,
And nothing to give.
I'm dying partly to taste,
What my soul has already did.
I wish I could've let death find me,
While I was still alive.

57. MY ELYSIAN PLAIN

Somedays I wanna fly
to the place I'll find elysian
away from the crowd
somewhere deep like
a burrow in the ground
As of know there's no more
hope and passion left in me
I'm living life Only because
I want to fulfil my death-dream
Everyday I wake up
And I want it to be the D-day
But every night I sleep in
hoping the same for the next day
I'm trying to lit the spark
in all the things I do
but everything is burning
me into ashes
And it feels so Ruth
I'm crumbling inside
Day by day
I hope to find my elysian plain
before I lay straight

58. PERFECT STONE

These loud whispers
that echoe in my mind
Makes it hard to live and fight
In hopes to redeem
my past and release my future
I'm marking my stone tonight
a grim truth
I just realised
My mortal scars
will not be there tonight
My stone encapsulates
the sorrow of yesterday,
Today and tomorrow
A plain block
Kept on my tomb
as everything dies with the root

www.ingramcontent.com/pod-product-compliance
Lightning Source LLC
LaVergne TN
LVHW041235150826
845673LV00008B/2390

* 9 7 9 8 8 9 6 7 3 5 8 4 7 *